Peter Goes

Fearless

an illustrated list of phobias

Lannoo

Ablutophobia

Fear of washing or bathing.

Automysophobia

Fear of being dirty.

Bromidrophobia – Bromidrosiphobia

Fear of body smells.

Acarophobia

Fear of itching or of the insects that cause itching.

Cnidophobia

Fear of stings.

Entomophobia – Insectophobia

Fear of insects.

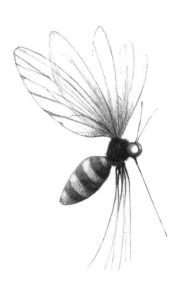

Acerophobia

Fear of sourness.

Achluophobia – Myctophobia – Scotophobia

Fear of darkness.

Lepidopterophobia

Fear of butterflies and moths.

Mottephobia

Fear of moths.

Acousticophobia

Fear of noise.

Acrophobia – Altophobia – Hypsiphobia

Fear of heights.

Batophobia

Fear of heights or being close to high buildings.

Illyngophobia

Fear of feeling dizzy when looking down.

Aeroacrophobia

Fear of open high places.

Bovinophobia

Fear of cattle.

Christougenniatiko Dentrophobia

Fear of Christmas trees.

Aeronausiphobia

Fear of vomiting due to airsickness.

Emetophobia

Fear of vomiting.

Olfactophobia – Osmophobia – Osphresiophobia

Fear of smells.

Aerophobia – Aviatophobia – Aviophobia

Fear of flying.

Cherophobia

Fear of happiness.

Scriptophobia

Fear of writing in public.

Tachophobia

Fear of speed.

Agliophobia – Algophobia – Odynophobia

Fear of pain.

Ankylophobia

Fear of immobility of a joint.

Asthenophobia

Fear of fainting or weakness.

Stenophobia

Fear of narrow things or places.

Agoraphobia – Demophobia

*Fear of open spaces or of being in crowded, public places.
Fear of leaving a safe place. Fear of unfamiliar environments.*

Anthrophobia – Anthropophobia

Fear of people or society.

Agrizoophobia

Fear of wild animals.

Diokophobia

Fear of being chased.

Lupophobia

Fear of wolves or werewolves.

Agyrophobia – Dromophobia

Fear of streets or crossing the street.

Ambulophobia – Stasibasiphobia – Stasiphobia

Fear of standing or walking.

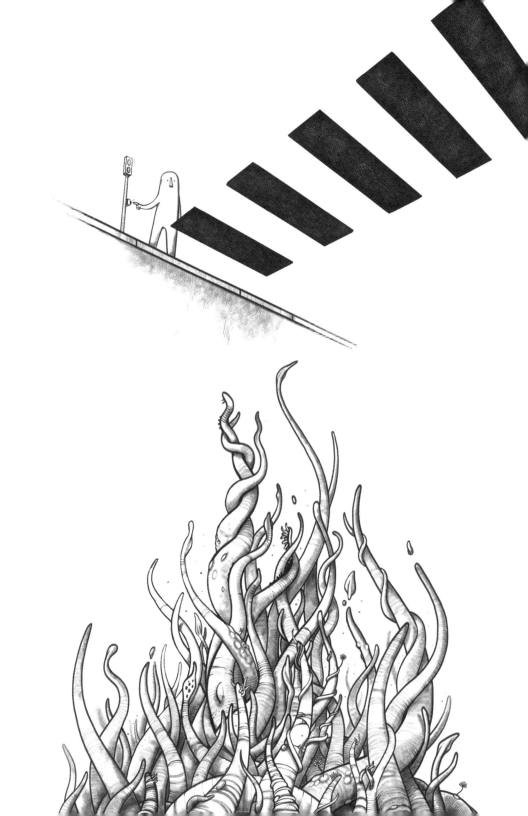

Aichmophobia

Fear of sharp objects.

Enetophobia

Fear of pins.

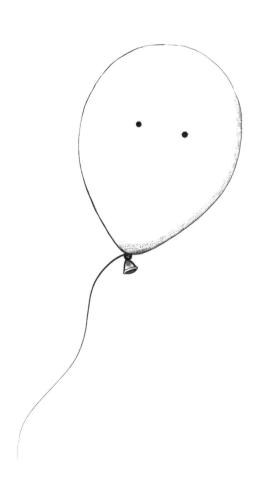

Ailurophobia – Elurophobia
Felinophobia – Gatophobia

Fear of cats.

Amychophobia

Fear of scratches or being scratched.

Cathisophobia – Kathisophobia – Thaasophobia

Fear of sitting.

Albuminurophobia

Fear of kidney disease.

Cardiophobia

Fear of a heart attack.

Geniophobia

Fear of chins.

Genuphobia

Fear of knees.

Ithyphallophobia – Medorthophobia – Phallophobia

Fear of an erect penis.

Tomophobia

Fear of surgical operations.

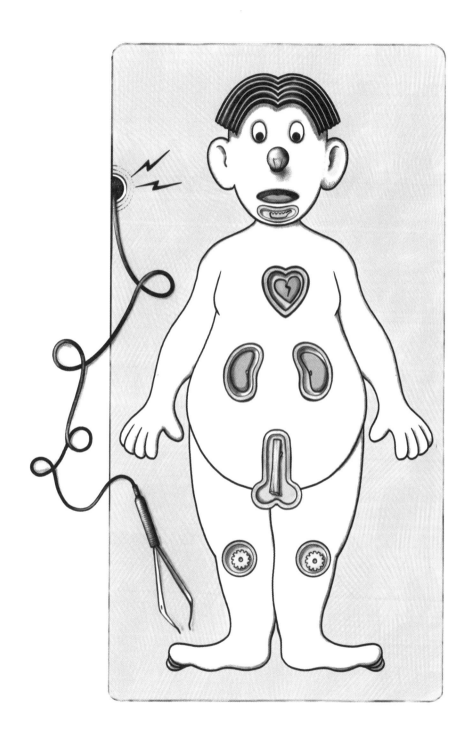

Alektorophobia

Fear of chickens.

Kalampokiphobia

Fear of corn.

Alliumphobia

Fear of garlic.

Argyrophobia

Fear of silvery things, silverware.

Eosophobia – Phengophobia

Fear of dawn or daylight.

Heliophobia

Fear of the sun.

Staurophobia

Fear of crosses or crucifixes.

Allodoxaphobia

Fear of opinions.

Doxophobia

Fear of expressing opinions or of receiving praise.

Ideophobia

Fear of ideas.

Visiolibriphobia

Fear of Facebook.

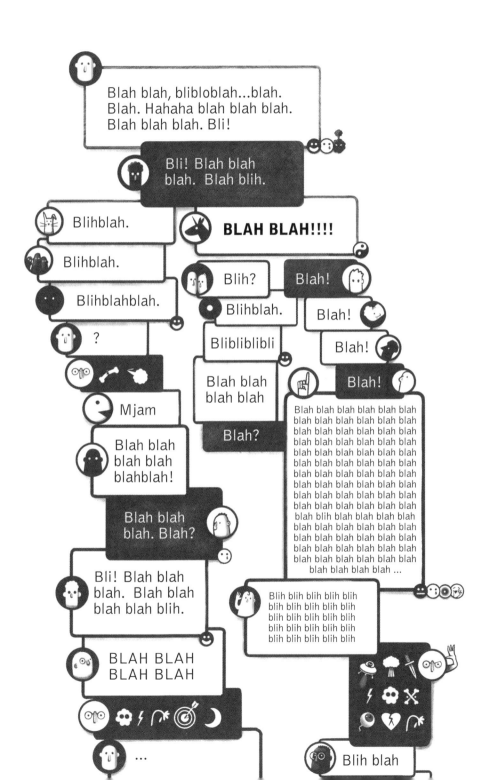

Amathophobia – Koniophobia

Fear of dust.

Chiroptophobia

Fear of bats.

Sciaphobia – Sciophobia

Fear of shadows.

Amaxophobia – Hamaxophobia
Motorphobia – Ochophobia

Fear of riding in a car.
Fear of vehicles.

Dystychiphobia

Fear of accidents.

Hodophobia

Fear of road travel.

Anablephobia

Fear of looking up.

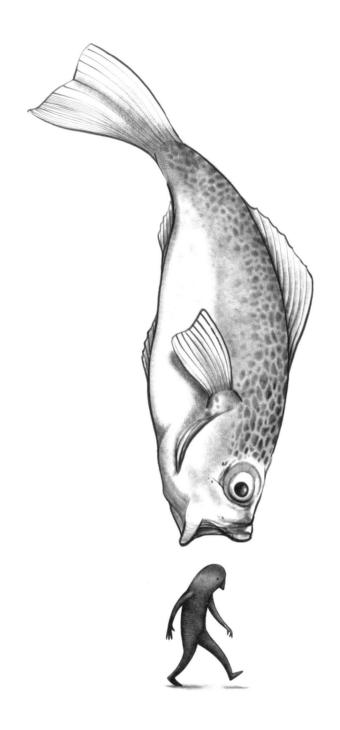

b   a

o   i

h

Ancraophobia – Anemo p

Fear of draughts or wind.

Kinesophobia – Kinetophobia

Fear of movement or motion.

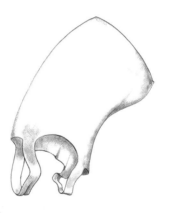

Androphobia – Arrhenphobia – Hominophobia

Fear of men.

Pogonophobia

Fear of beards.

Xyrophobia

Fear of razors.

Angrophobia

Fear of anger or of becoming angry.

Atychiphobia – Kakorrhaphiophobia

Fear of failure.

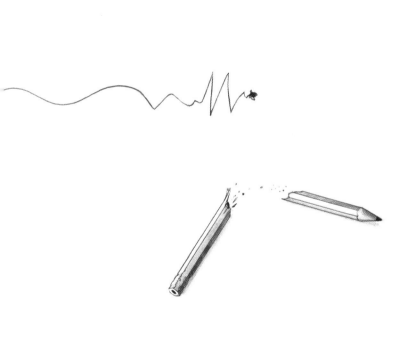

Anthophobia

Fear of flowers.

Apiphobia – Melissophobia

Fear of bees.

Biophobia

Fear of nature.

Antlophobia

Fear of floods.

Lilapsophobia

Fear of tornadoes or hurricanes.

Anuptaphobia

Fear of staying single.

Athazagoraphobia

Fear of being forgotton or ignored or forgetting.

Autophobia – Eremophobia
Isolophobia – Monophobia

Fear of being alone or isolated.

Soteriophobia

Fear of dependence on others.

Apeirophobia

Fear of infinity.

Astrophobia – Siderophobia

Fear of stars or celestial space.

Cometophobia

Fear of comets.

Ouranophobia – Uranophobia

Fear of heaven.

Selenophobia

Fear of the moon.

Spacephobia

Fear of outer space.

Aphenphosmphobia – Chiraptophobia
Haphephobia – Haptephobia

Fear of being touched.

Chirophobia

Fear of hands.

Eleutherophobia

Fear of freedom.

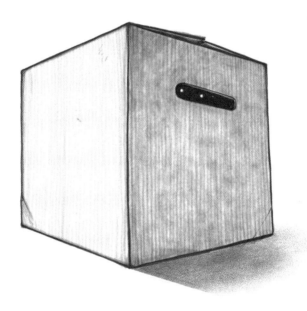

Apotemnophobia

Fear of amputations.

Aurophobia

Fear of gold.

Plutophobia

Fear of wealth.

Aquaphobia

Fear of water or of drowning.

Bathophobia

Fear of depths.

Arachibutyrophobia

Fear of peanut butter sticking to the roof of the mouth.

Geumaphobia

Fear of taste.

Arachnephobia – Arachnophobia

Fear of spiders.

Arsonphobia – Pyrophobia

Fear of fire.

Bibliophobia

Fear of books.

Epistemophobia – Gnosiophobia

Fear of knowledge.

Metrophobia

Fear of poetry.

Sophophobia

Fear of learning.

Astraphobia – Astrapophobia – Brontophobia
Ceraunophobia – Keraunophobia – Tonitrophobia

Fear of thunder and lightning.

Ligyrophobia – Phonophobia – Sonophobia

Fear of loud noises.

Selaphobia

Fear of light flashes.

Atephobia

Fear of ruins.

Tropophobia

Fear of moving or making changes.

Atomosophobia

Fear of atomic explosions.

Nucleomituphobia

Fear of nuclear weapons.

Aulophobia

Fear of flutes.

Muriphobia – Musophobia

Fear of mice or rats.

Autodysomophobia

Fear that one has a strong and unpleasant odour.

Bogyphobia

Fear of bogeys or the bogeyman.

Cacophobia

Fear of ugliness.

Dermatophobia – Dermatosiophobia

Fear of skin disease.

Dysmorphophobia

Fear of deformity.

Homichlophobia – Nebulaphobia

Fear of fog.

Automatonophobia

Fear of ventriloquist's dummies, animatronic creatures, wax statues, humanoid robots, or other figures designed to represent humans.

Isopterophobia

Fear of termites or other insects that eat wood.

Mythophobia

Fear of myths, stories or lying.

Pupaphobia

Fear of puppets.

Bacillophobia – Bacteriophobia
Germaphobia – Germophobia – Microbiophobia
Misophobia – Mysophobia – Verminophobia

Fear of contamination or germs.

Ballistophobia

Fear of missiles or bullets.

Hoplophobia

Fear of firearms.

Papaphobia

Fear of the pope or the papacy.

Barophobia

Fear of gravity.

Basiphobia – Basophobia

Fear of not being able to walk.
Fear of falling.

Kopophobia

Fear of fatigue.

Traumatophobia

Fear of injury.

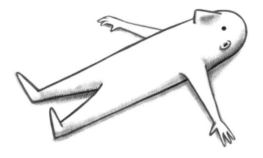

Bathmophobia – Climacophobia

Fear of stairs or slopes. Fear of climbing.

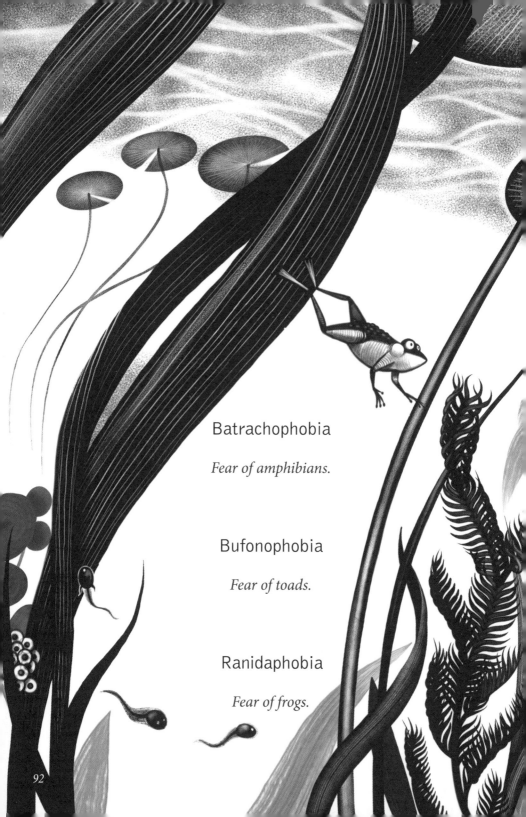

Batrachophobia

Fear of amphibians.

Bufonophobia

Fear of toads.

Ranidaphobia

Fear of frogs.

Belonephobia – Trypanophobia

Fear of needles or injections.

Tapinophobia

Fear of being contagious.

Vaccinophobia

Fear of vaccination.

Blennophobia – Myxophobia

Fear of slime.

Molluscophobia

Fear of slimy creatures, slugs or snails.

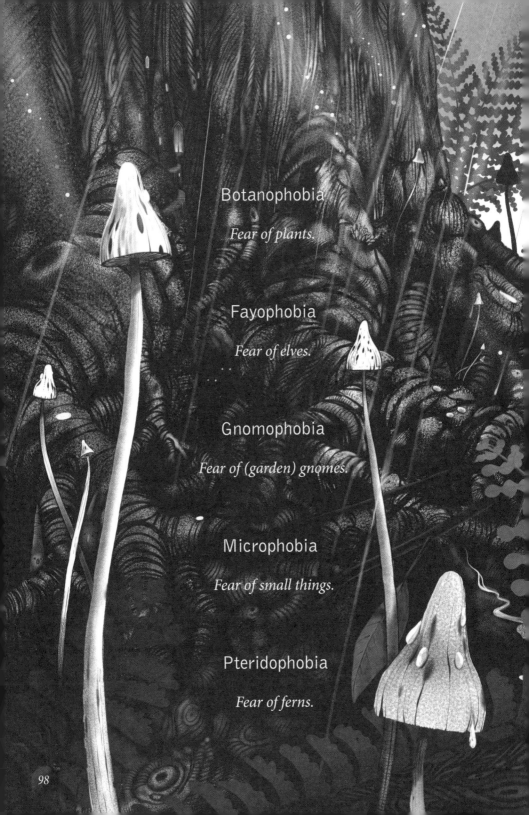

Botanophobia

Fear of plants.

Fayophobia

Fear of elves.

Gnomophobia

Fear of (garden) gnomes.

Microphobia

Fear of small things.

Pteridophobia

Fear of ferns.

Caligynephobia – Venustraphobia

Fear of beautiful women.

Eisoptrophobia

Fear of mirrors.

Zelophobia

Fear of jealousy.

Cancerophobia – Carcinophobia

Fear of cancer.

Chemophobia

Fear of chemicals or working with chemicals.

Panthophobia – Pathophobia

Fear of suffering or disease.

Pharmacophobia

Fear of taking medicine.

Radiophobia

Fear of radiation or x-rays.

Caramelaphobia

Fear of sweets.

Cucurbitophobia

Fear of pumpkins.

Diabetophobia

Fear of diabetes.

Saccharophobia

Fear of sugar or of sugary foods and drinks.

Samhainophobia

Fear of Halloween.

Carnophobia

Fear of meat.

Cibophobia – Sitiophobia – Sitophobia

Fear of food.

Lachanophobia

Fear of vegetables.

Obesophobia – Pocrescophobia

Fear of gaining weight.

Catagelophobia – Katagelophobia

Fear of being ridiculed.

Didaskaleinophobia – Scolionophobia

Fear of going to school.

Equinophobia – Hippophobia

Fear of horses, ponies, donkeys or mules.

Mastigophobia – Poinephobia

Fear of punishment.

Testophobia

Fear of taking tests.

Catapedaphobia

Fear of jumping from high and low places.

Decidophobia

Fear of making decisions.

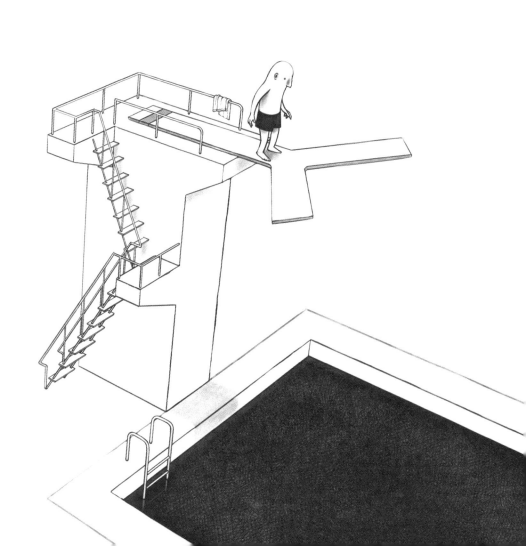

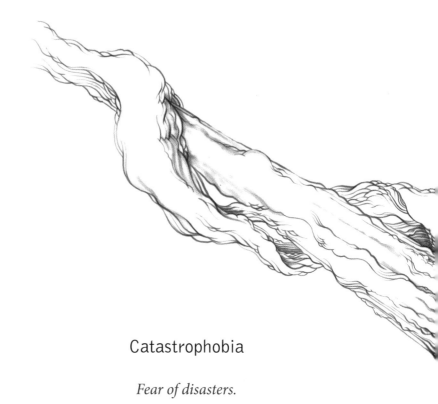

Catastrophobia

Fear of disasters.

Kosmikophobia

Fear of cosmic phenomena.

Meteorophobia

Fear of meteors.

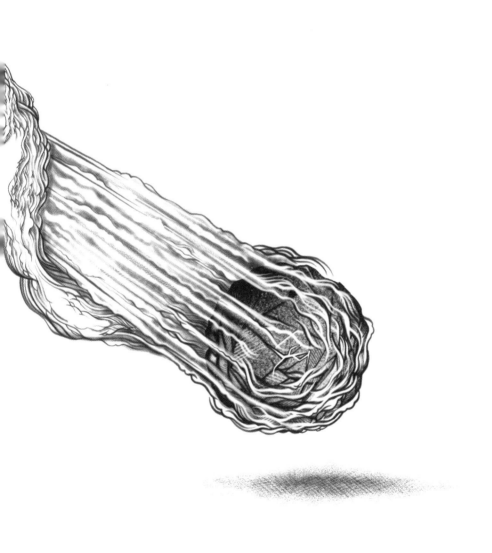

Cenosillicaphobia

Fear of an empty (beer, wine or cocktail) glass.

Diplophobia

Fear of double vision.

Dipsophobia – Methyphobia – Potophobia

Fear of drinking alcohol.

Oenophobia

Fear of wine.

Zythophobia

Fear of beer.

Chaetophobia – Hypertrichophobia
Trichopathophobia – Trichophobia

Fear of hair.

Parasitophobia

Fear of parasites.

Pediculophobia – Phthiriophobia

Fear of lice.

Chapodiphobia

Fear of octopuses.

Melanophobia

Fear of the colour black.

Cheimaphobia – Cheimatophobia
Frigophobia

Fear of cold.

Chionophobia

Fear of snow.

Cryophobia – Pagophobia

Fear of extreme cold, ice or frost.

Chorophobia

Fear of dancing.

Clinophobia

Fear of going to bed.

Koinoniphobia

Fear of rooms. Fear of rooms full of people.

Melophobia

Fear of music.

Chrematophobia – Chrometophobia

Fear of money.

Ghabhphobia

Fear of presents or gifts.

Kyphophobia

Fear of stooping.

Chronomentrophobia

Fear of clocks.

Chronophobia

Fear of time.

Claustrophobia – Cleisiophobia
Cleithrophobia – Clithrophobia

Fear of being trapped or confined in a small space.

Triskaidekaphobia

Fear of the number 13.

Paraskavedekatriaphobia

Fear of Friday the 13th.

Quadraphobia

Fear of the number four.

Quintaphobia

Fear of the number five.

Cleptophobia – Kleptophobia

Fear of stealing.

Cyclophobia

Fear of bicycles.

Harpaxophobia

Fear of being robbed.

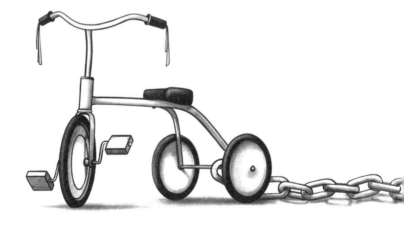

Consecotaleophobia

Fear of chopsticks.

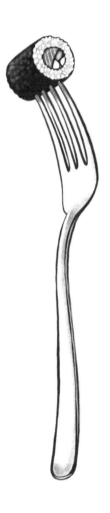

Coprastasophobia

Fear of constipation.

Coprophobia – Scatophobia

Fear of faeces.

Defecaloesiophobia

Fear of painful bowel movements.

Proctophobia – Rectophobia

Fear of rectums.

Rhypophobia

Fear of defecation.

Urophobia

Fear of urine or urinating.

Coulrophobia

Fear of clowns.

Gelotophobia

Fear of being laughed at.

Glossophobia

Fear of public speaking.

Psellismophobia

Fear of stuttering.

Theatrophobia

Fear of theatres.

Topophobia

Fear of certain places or situations, as in stage fright.

Counterphobia

*Compulsion to seek out a fearful situation
in an attempt to overcome the fear.*

Dikephobia

Fear of justice.

Scelerophobia

Fear of bad men or burglars.

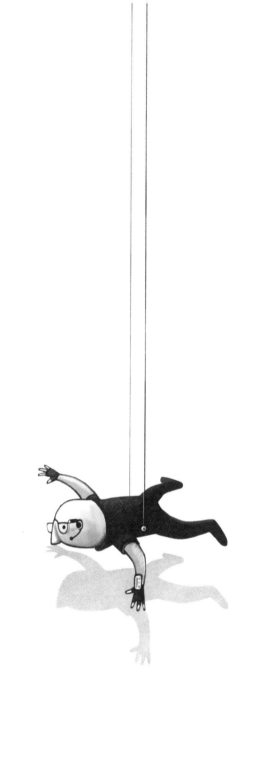

Crystallophobia

Fear of crystals or glass.

Hyalophobia – Hyelophobia – Nelophobia

Fear of glass.

Cyberphobia – Logizomechanophobia

Fear of computers or working on a computer.

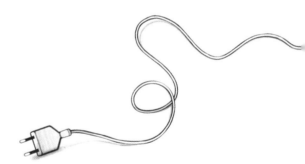

Electrophobia

Fear of electricity.

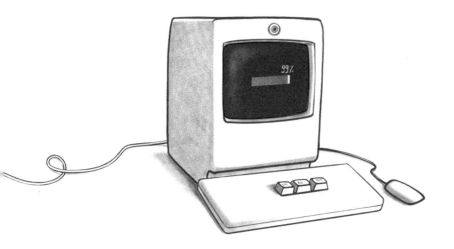

Cymophobia – Kymophobia

Fear of waves or wave-like motions.

Thalassophobia

Fear of the sea or large bodies of water.

Dendrophobia

Fear of trees.

Hylophobia

Fear of forests.

Mycophobia

Fear of mushrooms.

Noctiphobia

Fear of the night.

Nyctohylophobia.

Fear of dark, wooded areas or of forests at night.

Xylophobia

Fear of wooded areas.

Dentophobia

Fear of dentists.

Odontophobia

Fear of teeth or dental surgery.

Dextrophobia

Fear of objects to the right side of the body.

Gamophobia

Fear of marriage or commitment.

Levophobia

Fear of objects to the left side of the body.

Novercaphobia – Pentheraphobia

Fear of your step-mother.

Soceraphobia

Fear of your parents-in-law.

Doraphobia

Fear of fur or skins of animals.

Zemmiphobia

Fear of the great mole rat.

Zoophobia

Fear of animals.

Ecclesiophobia

Fear of churches.

Hagiophobia

Fear of saints or holy things.

Homilophobia

Fear of sermons.

Theologicophobia

Fear of theology.

Theophobia

Fear of gods or religion.

Ecophobia

Fear of home.

Nostophobia

Fear of returning home.

Orthophobia

Fear of property.

Erotophobia – Genophobia

Fear of sexual love or sexual questions.

Hedonophobia

Fear of feeling pleasure.

Malaxophobia – Sarmassophobia

Fear of love play.

Paraphobia

Fear of sexual perversion.

Philemaphobia – Philematophobia

Fear of kissing.

Philophobia

Fear of falling in love or being in love.

Pteronophobia

Fear of being tickled by feathers.

Eurotophobia – Kolpophobia

Fear of female genitalia.

Gymnophobia – Nudophobia

Fear of nudity.

Gynephobia – Gynophobia

Fear of women.

Mastrophobia

Fear of breasts.

Omphalophobia

Fear of belly buttons.

Galeophobia – Selachophobia

Fear of sharks.

Gephydrophobia – Gephyrophobia
Gephysrophobia

Fear of crossing bridges.

Hobophobia

Fear of vagrants or beggars.

Peniaphobia

Fear of poverty.

Potamophobia

Fear of rivers or running water.

Gerascophobia

Fear of growing old.

Gerontophobia

Fear of old people.

Peladophobia

Fear of bald people.

Phalacrophobia

Fear of becoming bald.

Rhytiphobia

Fear of getting wrinkles.

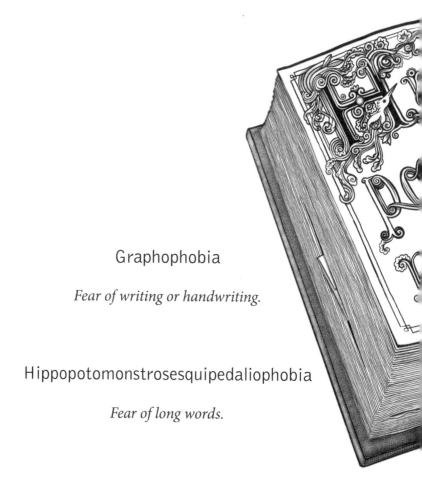

Graphophobia

Fear of writing or handwriting.

Hippopotomonstrosesquipedaliophobia

Fear of long words.

Logophobia – Verbophobia

Fear of words.

Hadephobia

Fear of hell.

170

Satanophobia

Fear of Satan.

Haemaphobia – Haematophobia – Haemophobia

Fear of blood.

Hypochondria – Nosemaphobia – Nosophobia

Fear of illness.

Iatrophobia

Fear of doctors or going to the doctor.

Meningitophobia

Fear of brain disease.

Nosocomephobia

Fear of hospitals.

Opiophobia

Fear of prescribing drugs, especially for pain relief.

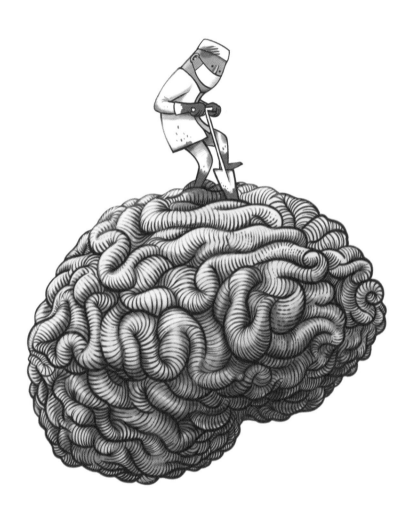

Herpetophobia

Fear of reptiles or crawly things.

Ophidiophobia

Fear of snakes.

Hexakosioihexekontahexaphobia

Fear of the number 666.

Hierophobia

Fear of priests or sacred things.

Ichthyophobia

Fear of fish.

Iophobia – Toxicophobia
Toxiphobia – Toxophobia

Fear of poison or of being poisoned.

Mageirocophobia

Fear of cooking.

Wiccaphobia

Fear of witches or witchcraft.

Kainolophobia – Kainophobia

Fear of anything new or of a novelty.

Mechanophobia

Fear of machines.

Metallophobia

Fear of metal.

Metathesiophobia

Fear of changes.

Prosophobia

Fear of progress.

Technophobia

Fear of technology.

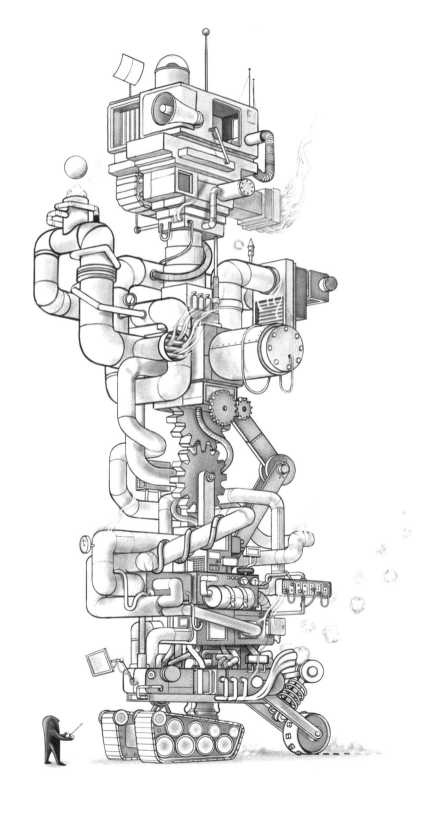

Kinemortophobia

Fear of zombies.

Necrophobia – Thanatophobia – Thantophobia

Fear of dead things, death or dying.

Placophobia

Fear of tombstones.

Scoleciphobia

Fear of worms.

Seplophobia

Fear of decaying matter.

Taphephobia – Taphophobia

*Fear of being buried alive
or of cemeteries.*

Leukophobia

Fear of the colour white.

Papyrophobia

Fear of paper.

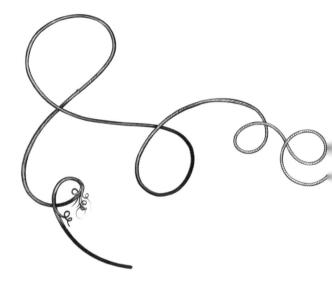

Linonophobia

Fear of string.

Merinthophobia

Fear of being bound or tied up.

Textophobia

Fear of certain fabrics.

Lockiophobia – Maieusiophobia
Parturiphobia – Tocophobia

Fear of pregnancy or childbirth.

Paediophobia

Fear of dolls.

Paedophobia

Fear of children.

Parthenophobia

Fear of virgins or young girls.

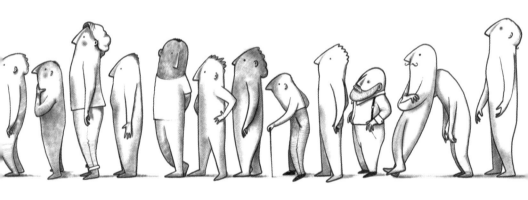

Macrophobia

Fear of long waits.

Telochronophobia

Fear of running out of time.

Megalophobia

Fear of large things.

Podophobia

Fear of feet.

Myrmecophobia

Fear of ants.

Phyllophobia

Fear of leaves.

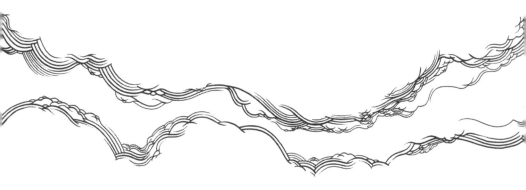

Nephophobia

Fear of clouds.

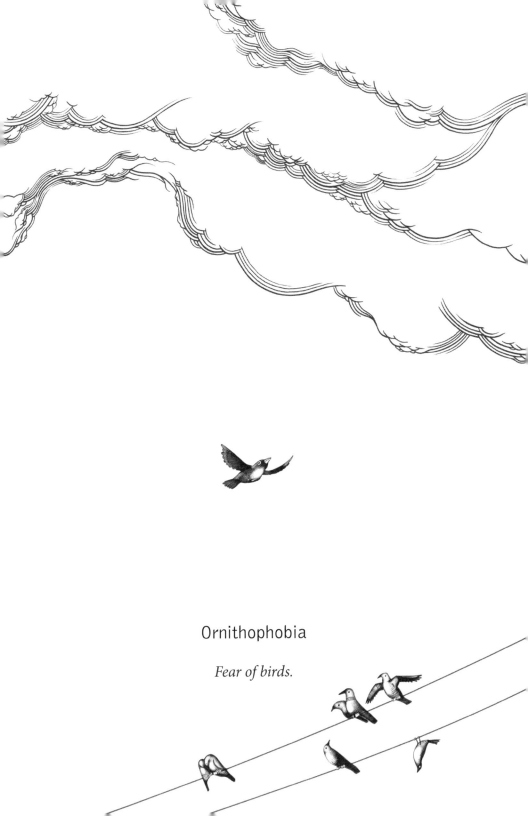

Ornithophobia

Fear of birds.

Octophobia

Fear of the number 8.

Phronemophobia

Fear of thinking.

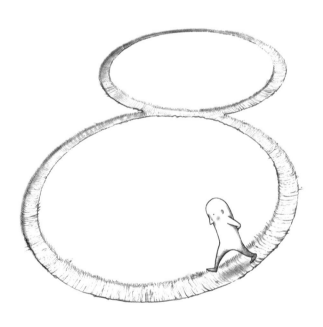

Ombrophobia – Pluviophobia

Fear of rain.

Pellebaphobia – Umbrellaphobia

Fear of umbrellas.

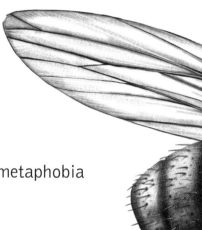

Ommatophobia – Ommetaphobia

Fear of eyes.

Ophthalmophobia – Scopophobia
Scoptophobia

Fear of being stared at.

Optophobia

Fear of opening one's eyes.

Scotomaphobia

Fear of blindness.

Oneirogmophobia

Fear of wet dreams.

Oneirophobia

Fear of dreams.

Somniphobia

Fear of sleep.

Phagophobia

Fear of swallowing or of eating or of being eaten.

Phasmophobia – Pneumatiphobia – Spectrophobia

Fear of spirits or ghosts.

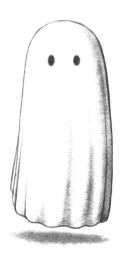

Politicophobia

Fear of politics or politicians.

Telephonophobia

Fear of telephones.

Tyrannophobia

Fear of tyrants and dictators.

Vestiphobia

Fear of clothing, especially uniforms.

Rhabdophobia

Fear of being beaten by a rod or of being severely criticized.
Fear of magic (wands).

Scyphophobia

Fear of jellyfish.

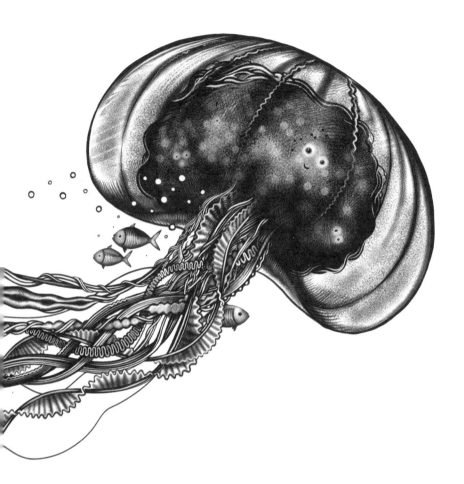

Spheksophobia

Fear of wasps.

Trypophobia

Fear of a pattern of small holes.

Xanthophobia

Fear of the colour yellow or the word yellow.

Strigiformophobia

Fear of owls.

T^remophobia

Fear of trembling.

Xenoglossophobia

Fear of foreign languages.

Xenophobia

*Fear of strangers or foreigners or
of anything that is strange or foreign.*

Zeusophobia

Fear of God or gods.

The sum of all fears

Panophobia *Fear of everything.* (Pantophobia)

A

Ablutophobia *Fear of washing or bathing.* 2
Acarophobia *Fear of itching or of the insects that cause itching.* 4
Acerophobia *Fear of sourness.* 6
Achluophobia *Fear of darkness.* (Myctophobia, Scotophobia) ... 8
Acousticophobia *Fear of noise.* 10
Acrophobia *Fear of heights.* (Altophobia, Hypsiphobia) 12
Aeroacrophobia *Fear of open high places.* 14
Aeronausiphobia *Fear of vomiting due to airsickness.* 16
Aerophobia *Fear of flying.* (Aviatophobia, Aviophobia) 18
Agateophobia *Fear of insanity.* (Dementophobia, Maniaphobia) ......
Agliophobia *Fear of pain.* (Algophobia, Odynophobia) 20
Agoraphobia *Fear of open spaces or of being in crowded,
public places. Fear of leaving a safe place. Fear of unfamiliar
environments.* (Demophobia) 22
Agraphobia *Fear of sexual abuse.* (Contreltophobia) ....
Agrizoophobia *Fear of wild animals.* 24
Agyrophobia *Fear of streets or crossing the street.* (Dromophobia) ... 26
Aichmophobia *Fear of sharp objects.* 28
Ailurophobia *Fear of cats.* (Elurophobia, Felinophobia,
Gatophobia) 30
Albuminurophobia *Fear of kidney disease.* 32
Alektorophobia *Fear of chickens.* 34
Alliumphobia *Fear of garlic.* 36
Allodoxaphobia *Fear of opinions.* 38
Amathophobia *Fear of dust.* (Koniophobia) 40
Amaxophobia *Fear of riding in a car. Fear of vehicles.*
(Hamaxophobia, Motorphobia, Ochophobia) 42
Ambulophobia *Fear of standing or walking.* (Stasibasiphobia,
Stasiphobia) 26

Amnesiphobia *Fear of amnesia.*

Amychophobia *Fear of scratches or being scratched.* 30

Anablephobia *Fear of looking up.* 44

Ancraophobia *Fear of draughts or wind.* (Anemophobia) 46

Androphobia *Fear of men.* (Arrhenphobia, Hominophobia) 48

Anginophobia *Fear of angina, choking or narrowness of the throat.*

Angrophobia *Fear of anger or of becoming angry.* 50

Ankylophobia *Fear of immobility of a joint.* 20

Anthophobia *Fear of flowers.* 52

Anthrophobia *Fear of people or society.* (Anthropophobia) 22

Antlophobia *Fear of floods.* 54

Anuptaphobia *Fear of staying single.* 56

Apeirophobia *Fear of infinity.* 58

Aphenphosmphobia *Fear of being touched.* (Chiraptophobia,
Haphephobia, Haptephobia,) 60

Apiphobia *Fear of bees.* (Melissophobia) 52

Apotemnophobia *Fear of amputations.* 62

Aquaphobia *Fear of water or of drowning.* 64

Arachibutyrophobia *Fear of peanut butter sticking to the roof
of the mouth.* 66

Arachnephobia *Fear of spiders.* (Arachnophobia) 68

Arithmophobia *Fear of numbers.* (Numerophobia)

Argyrophobia *Fear of silvery things, silverware.* 36

Arsonphobia *Fear of fire.* (Pyrophobia) 70

Asthenophobia *Fear of fainting or weakness.* 20

Astraphobia *Fear of thunder and lightning.* (Astrapophobia,
Brontophobia, Ceraunophobia, Keraunophobia, Tonitrophobia) 72

Astrophobia *Fear of stars or celestial space.* (Siderophobia) 58

Asymmetriphobia *Fear of asymmetry.* (Asymmetrophobia)

Ataxiophobia *Fear of ataxia (muscular incoordination).*

Ataxophobia *Fear of disorder or untidiness.*

Atelophobia *Fear of imperfection.*

Atephobia *Fear of ruins.* 74

Athazagoraphobia *Fear of being forgotton or ignored or forgetting.* 56

Atomosophobia *Fear of atomic explosions.* 76

Atychiphobia *Fear of failure.* (Kakorrhaphiophobia) 50

Aulophobia *Fear of flutes.* 78

Aurophobia *Fear of gold.* 62
Auroraphobia *Fear of northern lights.* ....
Autodysomophobia *Fear that one has a strong and unpleasant*
odour. 80
Automatonophobia *Fear of ventriloquist's dummies, animatronic*
creatures, wax statues, humanoid robots, or other figures designed
to represent humans. 82
Automysophobia *Fear of being dirty.* 2
Autophobia *Fear of being alone or isolated.* (Eremophobia,
Isolophobia, Monophobia) 56

B

Bacillophobia *Fear of contamination or germs.* (Bacteriophobia,
Germaphobia, Germophobia, Microbiophobia, Misophobia,
Mysophobia, Verminophobia) 84
Ballistophobia *Fear of missiles or bullets.* 86
Barophobia *Fear of gravity.* 88
Basiphobia *Fear of not being able to walk. Fear of falling.*
(Basophobia) 88
Bathmophobia *Fear of stairs or slopes. Fear of climbing*
(Climacophobia) 90
Bathophobia *Fear of depths.* 64
Batophobia *Fear of heights or being close to high buildings.* 12
Batrachophobia *Fear of amphibians.* 92
Belonephobia *Fear of needles or injections.* (Trypanophobia) 94
Bibliophobia *Fear of books.* 70
Biophobia *Fear of nature.* 52
Blennophobia *Fear of slime.* (Myxophobia) 96
Bogyphobia *Fear of bogeys or the bogeyman.* 80
Botanophobia *Fear of plants.* 98
Bovinophobia *Fear of cattle.* 14
Bromidrophobia *Fear of body smells.* (Bromidrosiphobia) 2
Bufonophobia *Fear of toads.* 92

C

Cacophobia *Fear of ugliness.* 80
Caligynephobia *Fear of beautiful women.* (Venustraphobia) 100
Cancerophobia *Fear of cancer.* (Carcinophobia) 102
Caramelaphobia *Fear of sweets.* 104
Cardiophobia *Fear of a heart attack.* 32
Carnophobia *Fear of meat.* 106
Catagelophobia *Fear of being ridiculed.* (Katagelophobia) 108
Catapedaphobia *Fear of jumping from high or low places.* 110
Catastrophobia *Fear of disasters.* 112
Cathisophobia *Fear of sitting.* (Kathisophobia, Thaasophobia) 30
Cenosillicaphobia *Fear of an empty (beer, wine or cocktail) glass.* ... 114
Chaetophobia *Fear of hair.* (Hypertrichophobia,
Trichopathophobia, Trichophobia) 116
Chapodiphobia *Fear of octopuses.* 118
Cheimaphobia *Fear of cold.* (Cheimatophobia, Frigophobia) 120
Chemophobia *Fear of chemicals or working with chemicals.* 102
Cherophobia *Fear of happiness.* 18
Chionophobia *Fear of snow.* 120
Chirophobia *Fear of hands.* 60
Chiroptophobia *Fear of bats.* 40
Christougenniatiko Dentrophobia *Fear of Christmas trees.* 15
Cholerophobia *Fear of anger or fear of cholera.*
Chorophobia *Fear of dancing.* 122
Chrematophobia *Fear of money.* (Chrometophobia) 124
Chromophobia *Fear of colours.* (Chromatophobia)
Chronomentrophobia *Fear of clocks.* 126
Chronophobia *Fear of time.* 126
Cibophobia *Fear of food.* (Sitiophobia, Sitophobia) 106
Claustrophobia *Fear of being trapped or confined in a small space.*
(Cleisiophobia, Cleithrophobia, Clithrophobia) 128
Cleptophobia *Fear of stealing.* (Kleptophobia) 130
Clinophobia *Fear of going to bed.* 122
Cnidophobia *Fear of stings.* 4

Coimetrophobia *Fear of cemeteries.* ....
Coitophobia *Fear of coitus.* ....
Cometophobia *Fear of comets.* 58
Coprastasophobia *Fear of constipation.* 134
Coprophobia *Fear of faeces.* (Scatophobia) 134
Consecotaleophobia *Fear of chopsticks.* 132
Coulrophobia *Fear of clowns.* 136
Counterphobia *Compulsion to seek out a fearful situation in an*
attempt to overcome the fear. 138
Cremnophobia *Fear of precipices.* ....
Cucurbitophobia *Fear of pumpkins.* 104
Cryophobia *Fear of extreme cold, ice or frost.* (Pagophobia) 120
Crystallophobia *Fear of crystals or glass.* 140
Cyberphobia *Fear of computers or working on a computer.*
(Logizomechanophobia) 142
Cyclophobia *Fear of bicycles.* 130
Cymophobia *Fear of waves or wave-like motions.* (Kymophobia) .. 144
Cynophobia *Fear of dogs or getting rabies from a dog.*
(Kynophobia) ....
Cyprianophobia *Fear of prostitutes or venereal disease.*
(Cypridophobia, Cyprinophobia, Cypriphobia) ....

D

Daemonophobia *Fear of demons.* (Demonophobia) ....
Decidophobia *Fear of making decisions.* 110
Defecaloesiophobia *Fear of painful bowel movements.* 134
Deipnophobia *Fear of dining or dinner conversations.* ....
Dendrophobia *Fear of trees.* 146
Dentophobia *Fear of dentists.* 148
Dermatophobia *Fear of skin disease.* (Dermatosiophobia) 80
Dextrophobia *Fear of objects to the right side of the body.* 150
Diabetophobia *Fear of diabetes.* 104

Didaskaleinophobia *Fear of going to school.* (Scolionophobia) 108
Dikephobia *Fear of justice.* 138
Dinophobia *Fear of dizziness or whirlpools.* ....
Diokophobia *Fear of being chased.* 24
Diplophobia *Fear of double vision.* 114
Dipsophobia *Fear of drinking alcohol.* (Methyphobia,
Potophobia) 114
Dishabiliophobia *Fear of undressing in front of someone.* ....
Disposophobia *Fear of throwing stuff out.* ....
Domatophobia *Fear of houses or being in a house.* (Eicophobia,
Oikophobia) ....
Doraphobia *Fear of fur or skins of animals.* 152
Doxophobia *Fear of expressing opinions or of receiving praise.* 38
Dysmorphophobia *Fear of deformity.* 80
Dystychiphobia *Fear of accidents.* 42

E

Ecclesiophobia *Fear of churches.* 154
Ecophobia *Fear of home.* 156
Eisoptrophobia *Fear of mirrors.* 100
Electrophobia. *Fear of electricity.* 142
Eleutherophobia *Fear of freedom.* 60
Emetophobia *Fear of vomiting.* 16
Enetophobia *Fear of pins.* 28
Enochlophobia *Fear of crowds.* ....
Enosiophobia *Fear of criticism or committing a sin.* (Enissophobia) ....
Entomophobia *Fear of insects.* (Insectophobia) 4
Eosophobia *Fear of dawn or daylight.* (Phengophobia) 36
Ephebiphobia *Fear of teenagers.* ....
Epistaxiophobia *Fear of nosebleeds.* ....
Epistemophobia *Fear of knowledge.* (Gnosiophobia) 70

Equinophobia *Fear of horses, ponies, donkeys or mules.*
(Hippophobia).. 108
Ereuthophobia *Fear of blushing.* (Erythrophobia, Erytophobia)........
Ergasiophobia *Fear of labour.* (Ergophobia, Ponophobia)................
Erotophobia *Fear of sexual love or sexual questions.* ....
(Genophobia) 158
Euphobia *Fear of hearing good news.* ....
Eurotophobia *Fear of female genitalia.* (Kolpophobia) 160

F – G

Fayophobia *Fear of elves.*.. 98
Febriphobia *Fear of fever.* (Fibriphobia, Fibriophobia,
Pyrexiophobia) ....
Galeophobia *Fear of sharks.* (Selachophobia) 162
Gamophobia *Fear of marriage or commitment.* 150
Geliophobia *Fear of laughter.* 136
Gelotophobia *Fear of being laughed at.*................................. 136
Geniophobia *Fear of chins.*.. 32
Genuphobia *Fear of knees.* 32
Gephydrophobia *Fear of crossing bridges.* (Gephyrophobia,
Gephysrophobia) 164
Gerascophobia *Fear of growing old.* 166
Gerontophobia *Fear of old people.* 166
Geumaphobia *Fear of taste.* (Geumophobia) 66
Ghabhphobia *Fear of presents or gifts.* 124
Glossophobia *Fear of public speaking.* 136
Gnomophobia *Fear of (garden) gnomes.*................................. 98
Graphophobia *Fear of writing or handwriting.* 168
Gymnophobia *Fear of nudity.* (Nudophobia) 160
Gynephobia *Fear of women.* (Gynophobia) 160

H

Hadephobia *Fear of hell.* 170

Haemaphobia *Fear of blood.* (Haematophobia, Haemophobia) 172

Hagiophobia *Fear of saints or holy things.* 154

Hamartophobia *Fear of committing an error, sin or crime.*
(Peccatophobia) ....

Harpaxophobia *Fear of being robbed.* 130

Hedonophobia *Fear of feeling pleasure.* 158

Heliophobia *Fear of the sun.* 36

Hellenologophobia *Fear of Greek terms or complex scientific*
terminology. ....

Helminthophobia *Fear of being infested with worms.* ....

Heresyphobia *Fear of official doctrine or of radical deviation.*
(Hereiophobia) ....

Herpetophobia *Fear of reptiles or crawly things.* 174

Heterophobia *Fear of the opposite sex.* (Sexophobia) ....

Hexakosioihexekontahexaphobia *Fear of the number 666.* 176

Hierophobia *Fear of priests or sacred things.* 177

Hippopotomonstrosesquipedaliophobia *Fear of long words.* 168

Hobophobia *Fear of vagrants or beggars.* 164

Hodophobia *Fear of road travel.* 42

Hormephobia *Fear of shock.* ....

Homichlophobia *Fear of fog.* (Nebulaphobia) 80

Homilophobia *Fear of sermons.* 154

Hoplophobia *Fear of firearms.* 86

Hydrophobia *Fear of water related to rabies infection.* ....

Hydrophobophobia *Fear of rabies.* (Lyssophobia) ....

Hyalophobia *Fear of glass.* (Hyelophobia, Nelophobia) 140

Hygrophobia *Fear of liquids, dampness, or moisture.* ....

Hylephobia *Fear of materialism or the fear of epilepsy.* ....

Hylophobia *Fear of forests.* 146

Hypengyophobia *Fear of responsibility.* (Hypegiaphobia) ....

Hypnophobia *Fear of sleep or of being hypnotized.* ....

Hypochondria *Fear of illness.* (Nosemaphobia, Nosophobia) 172

I – J

Iatrophobia *Fear of doctors or going to the doctor.* 172
Ichthyophobia *Fear of fish.* 179
Ideophobia *Fear of ideas.* 38
Illyngophobia *Fear of feeling dizzy when looking down.* 12
Iophobia *Fear of poison or of being poisoned.* (Toxicophobia, Toxiphobia, Toxophobia) 180
Isopterophobia *Fear of termites or other insects that eat wood.* 82
Ithyphallophobia *Fear of an erect penis.* (Medorthophobia, Phallophobia) 32

K – L

Kainolophobia *Fear of anything new or of a novelty.* (Kainophobia) 182
Kalampokiphobia *Fear of corn.* 34
Katsaridaphobia *Fear of cockroaches.*
Kenophobia *Fear of voids or empty spaces.*
Kinemortophobia *Fear of zombies.* 184
Kinesophobia *Fear of movement or motion.* (Kinetophobia) 46
Koinoniphobia *Fear of rooms. Fear of rooms full of people.* 122
Kopophobia *Fear of fatigue.* 88
Kosmikophobia *Fear of cosmic phenomena.* 112
Koumpounophobia *Fear of buttons.*
Kyphophobia *Fear of stooping.* 124
Lachanophobia *Fear of vegetables.* 106
Laliophobia *Fear of speaking.* (Lalophobia)
Lepidopterophobia *Fear of butterflies and moths.* 8
Lepraphobia *Fear of leprosy.* (Leprophobia)
Leukophobia *Fear of the colour white.* 186

Levophobia *Fear of things to the left side of the body.* 150
Ligyrophobia *Fear of loud noises.* (Phonophobia, Sonophobia) 72
Lilapsophobia *Fear of tornadoes or hurricanes.* 54
Limnophobia *Fear of lakes.*
Linonophobia *Fear of string.* 188
Liticaphobi *Fear of lawsuits.*
Lockiophobia *Fear of pregnancy or childbirth.* (Maieusiophobia, Parturiphobia, Tocophobia) 190
Logophobia *Fear of words.* (Verbophobia) 168
Luiphobia *Fear of lues, particularly syphilis.*
Lupophobia *Fear of wolves or werewolves.* 24
Lutraphobia *Fear of otters.*

M

Macrophobia *Fear of long waits.* 192
Mageirocophobia *Fear of cooking.* 180
Malaxophobia *Fear of love play.* (Sarmassophobia) 158
Mastigophobia *Fear of punishment.* (Poinephobia) 108
Mastrophobia *Fear of breasts.* 160
Mechanophobia *Fear of machines.* 182
Medomalacuphobia *Fear of losing an erection.*
Megalophobia *Fear of large things.* 194
Melanophobia *Fear of the colour black.* 119
Melophobia *Fear of music.* 122
Meningitophobia *Fear of brain disease.* 172
Menophobia *Fear of menstruation.*
Merinthophobia *Fear of being bound or tied up.* 188
Metallophobia *Fear of metal.* 182
Metathesiophobia *Fear of changes.* 182
Meteorophobia *Fear of meteors.* 112
Metrophobia *Fear of poetry.* 70
Microphobia *Fear of small things.* 98

Mnemophobia *Fear of memories.* ....
Molysmophobia *Fear of dirt or contamination.* (Molysomophobia) ....
Monopathophobia *Fear of definite disease.* ....
Mottephobia *Fear of moths.* 8
Molluscophobia *Fear of slimy creatures, slugs or snails.* 96
Muriphobia *Fear of mice or rats.* (Musophobia) 78
Mycophobia *Fear of mushrooms.* 146
Myrmecophobia *Fear of ants.* 196
Mythophobia *Fear of myths, stories or lying.* 82

N

Necrophobia *Fear of death or dying.* (Thanatophobia,
Thantophobia) 184
Neopharmaphobia *Fear of new drugs.* ....
Neophobia *Fear of anything new.* ....
Nephophobia *Fear of clouds.* 198
Noctiphobia *Fear of the night.* 146
Nomatophobia *Fear of names.* ....
Nosocomephobia *Fear of hospitals.* 172
Nostophobia *Fear of returning home.* 156
Novercaphobia *Fear of your step-mother.* (Pentheraphobia) 150
Nucleomituphobia *Fear of nuclear weapons.* 76
Nyctohylophobia *Fear of dark, wooded areas or of forests at night.* 146

O

Obesophobia *Fear of gaining weight.* (Pocrescophobia) 107
Ochlophobia *Fear of mob-like crowds.* ....
Octophobia *Fear of the number 8.* 200
Odontophobia *Fear of teeth or dental surgery.* 148
Oenophobia *Fear of wine.* 114
Olfactophobia *Fear of smells.* (Osmophobia, Osphresiophobia) 16
Ombrophobia *Fear of rain.* (Pluviophobia) 202
Ommatophobia *Fear of eyes.* (Ommetaphobia) 204
Omphalophobia *Fear of belly buttons.* 160
Oneirogmophobia *Fear of wet dreams.* 206
Oneirophobia *Fear of dreams.* 206
Onomatophobia *Fear of hearing a certain word or name.* ....
Ophidiophobia *Fear of snakes.* 174
Ophthalmophobia *Fear of being stared at.* (Scopophobia,
Scoptophobia) 204
Opiophobia *Fear of prescribing drugs, especially for pain relief.* 172
Optophobia *Fear of opening one's eyes.* 204
Ornithophobia *Fear of birds.* 199
Orthophobia *Fear of property.* 156
Ostraconophobia *Fear of shellfish.* ....
Ouranophobia *Fear of heaven.* (Uranophobia) 58

P

Paediophobia *Fear of dolls.* 190
Paedophobia *Fear of children.* 190
Panthophobia *Fear of suffering or disease.* (Pathophobia) 102
Panophobia *Fear of everything.* (Pantophobia) ....
Papaphobia *Fear of the pope or the papacy.* 86

Papyrophobia *Fear of paper.* 186
Paralipophobia *Fear of neglecting duty or responsibility.*
Paraphobia *Fear of sexual perversion.* 158
Parasitophobia *Fear of parasites.* 116
Paraskavedekatriaphobia *Fear of Friday the 13th.* 128
Parthenophobia *Fear of virgins or young girls.* 190
Patroiophobia *Fear of heredity.*
Pediculophobia *Fear of lice.* (Phthiriophobia) 116
Peladophobia *Fear of bald people.* 166
Pellebaphobia *Fear of umbrellas.* (Umbrellaphobia) 202
Peniaphobia *Fear of poverty.* 164
Phagophobia *Fear of swallowing or of eating or of being eaten.* 208
Phalacrophobia *Fear of becoming bald.* 166
Pharmacophobia *Fear of taking medicine.* 102
Phasmophobia *Fear of spirits or ghosts.* (Pneumatiphobia,
Spectrophobia) 210
Philemaphobia *Fear of kissing.* (Philematophobia) 158
Philophobia *Fear of falling in love or being in love.* 158
Philosophobia *Fear of philosophy.*
Phobophobia *Fear of phobias.*
Photoaugliaphobia *Fear of glaring lights.*
Photophobia *Fear of light.*
Phronemophobia *Fear of thinking.* 200
Phthisiophobia *Fear of tuberculosis.* (Tuberculophobia)
Phyllophobia *Fear of leaves.* 197
Placophobia *Fear of tombstones.* 184
Plutophobia *Fear of wealth.* 62
Pnigophobia *Fear of choking of being smothered.* (Pnigerophobia)
Pogonophobia *Fear of beards.* 48
Poliosophobia *Fear of contracting poliomyelitis.*
Politicophobia *Fear of politics or politicians.* 212
Polyphobia *Fear of many things.*
Porphyrophobia *Fear of the colour purple.*
Potamophobia *Fear of rivers or running water.* 164
Podophobia *Fear of feet.* 195
Pharmacophobia *Fear of drugs.*
Proctophobia *Fear of rectums.* (Rectophobia) 134
Prosophobia *Fear of progress.* 182

Psellismophobia *Fear of stuttering.* 136
Psychophobia *Fear of mind.*
Pteridophobia *Fear of ferns.* 98
Pteronophobia *Fear of being tickled by feathers.* 159
Pupaphobia *Fear of puppets.* 82

Q – R – S

Quadraphobia *Fear of the number four.* 128
Quadriplegiphobia *Fear of quadriplegics or of becoming a quadriplegic.*
Quintaphobia *Fear of the number five.* 128
Radiophobia *Fear of radiation or x-rays.* 102
Ranidaphobia *Fear of frogs.* 92
Rhabdophobia *Fear of being beaten by a rod or of being severely criticized. Fear of magic (wands).* 214
Rhypophobia *Fear of defecation.* 134
Rhytiphobia *Fear of getting wrinkles.* 166
Rupophobia *Fear of dirt or filth.*
Saccharophobia *Fear of sugar or of sugary foods and drinks.* 104
Samhainophobia *Fear of Halloween.* 104
Satanophobia *Fear of Satan.* 171
Scabiophobia *Fear of scabies.*
Scelerophobia *Fear of bad men or burglars.* 138
Sciaphobia *Fear of shadows. (Sciophobia)* 40
Scoleciphobia *Fear of worms.* 184
Scotomaphobia *Fear of blindness.* 204
Scriptophobia *Fear of writing in public.* 18
Scyphophobia *Fear of jellyfish.* 216
Seismophobia *Fear of earthquakes.*
Selaphobia *Fear of light flashes.* 72
Selenophobia *Fear of the moon.* 58
Seplophobia *Fear of decaying matter.* 184
Siderodromophobia *Fear of trains, railroads or train travel.*

Sinistrophobia *Fear of things to the left or left-handedness.* ....

Soceraphobia *Fear of your parents-in-law.* 150

Socialphobia *Fear of being evaluated negatively in social situations.* ......

Sociophobia *Fear of society or people in general.* ....

Somniphobia *Fear of falling asleep.* 206

Sophophobia *Fear of learning.* 70

Soteriophobia *Fear of dependence on others.* 56

Spacephobia *Fear of outer space.* 58

Spheksophobia *Fear of wasps.* 218

Staurophobia *Fear of crosses or crucifixes.* 36

Stenophobia *Fear of narrow things or places.* 20

Strigiformophobia *Fear of owls.* 220

Suriphobia *Fear of mice.* ....

Symbolophobia *Fear of symbolism.* ....

Symmetrophobia *Fear of symmetry.* ....

Syngenesophobia *Fear of relatives.* ....

Syphilophobia *Fear of syphilis.* ....

T

Tachophobia *Fear of speed.* 18

Taeniophobia *Fear of tapeworms.* (Teniophobia) ....

Taphephobia *Fear of being buried alive or of cemeteries.*
(Taphophobia) 185

Tapinophobia *Fear of being contagious.* 94

Taurophobia *Fear of bulls.* ....

Technophobia *Fear of technology.* 182

Teleophobia *Fear of definite plans or religious ceremony.* ....

Telephonophobia *Fear of telephones.* 212

Telochronophobia *Fear of running out of time.* 193

Teratophobia *Fear of bearing a deformed child or fear of monsters
or deformed people.* ....

Testophobia *Fear of taking tests.* 108

Tetanophobia *Fear of lockjaw, tetanus.* ....

Textophobia *Fear of certain fabrics.* 188
Thalassophobia *Fear of the sea or large bodies of water.* 145
Theatrophobia *Fear of theatres.* 136
Theologicophobia *Fear of theology.* 154
Theophobia *Fear of gods or religion.* 154
Thermophobia *Fear of heat.*
Tomophobia *Fear of surgical operations.* 32
Topophobia *Fear of certain places or situations, as in stage fright.* 136
Traumatophobia *Fear of injury.* 88
Tremophobia *Fear of trembling.* 222
Triskaidekaphobia *Fear of the number 13.* 128
Tropophobia *Fear of moving or making changes.* 74
Trypophobia *Fear of a pattern of small holes.* 218
Tyrannophobia *Fear of tyrants and dictators.* 213

U – V – W

Urophobia *Fear of urine or urinating.* 134
Vaccinophobia *Fear of vaccination.* 94
Vestiphobia *Fear of clothing, especially uniforms.* 213
Virginitiphobia *Fear of rape.*
Visiolibriphobia *Fear of Facebook.* 38
Vitricophobia *Fear of your step-father.*
Wiccaphobia *Fear of witches or witchcraft.* 180

X – Y – Z

Xanthophobia *Fear of the colour yellow or the word yellow.*............ 218
Xenoglossophobia *Fear of foreign languages.* 224
Xenophobia *Fear of strangers or foreigners or of anything that is*
strange or foreign. 224
Xerophobia *Fear of dryness.*...
Xylophobia *Fear of wooded areas.* 146
Xyrophobia *Fear of razors.* 48
Zelophobia *Fear of jealousy.*... 100
Zeusophobia *Fear of God or gods.*..................................... 226
Zemmiphobia *Fear of the great mole rat.* 152
Zoophobia *Fear of animals.* 152
Zythophobia *Fear of beer.*... 114

The list of phobias in this book is not complete and never will be. There is no official list of phobias, so clinicians and researchers create names for them as the need arises. This is typically done by combining a Greek (or Latin) name that describes the object of fear with the suffix of 'phobia'.

A phobia is an overwhelming fear of something that is unlikely to cause harm. The word comes from the Greek word *phobos*, which means 'fear' or 'horror'.

According to the DSM,* phobias typically fall within five general categories:

> fears related to animals (spiders, dogs, insects)
> fears related to the natural environment (heights, darkness)
> fears related to injury, or medical issues (choking, injections)
> fears related to specific situations (flying, using a lift)
> other (fear of drowning, falling, loud noises)

There are possible risks in labeling people who have anxieties. Human beings are complex creatures who have a wide variety of virtues and uncertainties.

*The Diagnostic and Statistical Manual of Mental Disorders published by the American Psychiatric Association for the classification of mental disorders.

For Ann, Sammes and Jan

Many thanks to all the fine people at Lannoo Publishers.

You can visit me at:
www.petergoes.com
www.instagram.com/goes.peter

Book design by the author
Entire contents copyright © 2022 by Peter Goes

©Lannoo Publishers, 2022
ISBN: 978 94 014 7376 7
NUR 400,640
D/2022/45/384

www.lannoopublishers.com
Subscribe to our newsletter for regular information on our publications and activities.